Bratislava Travel Highlights

Best Attractions & Experiences

Donald Harris

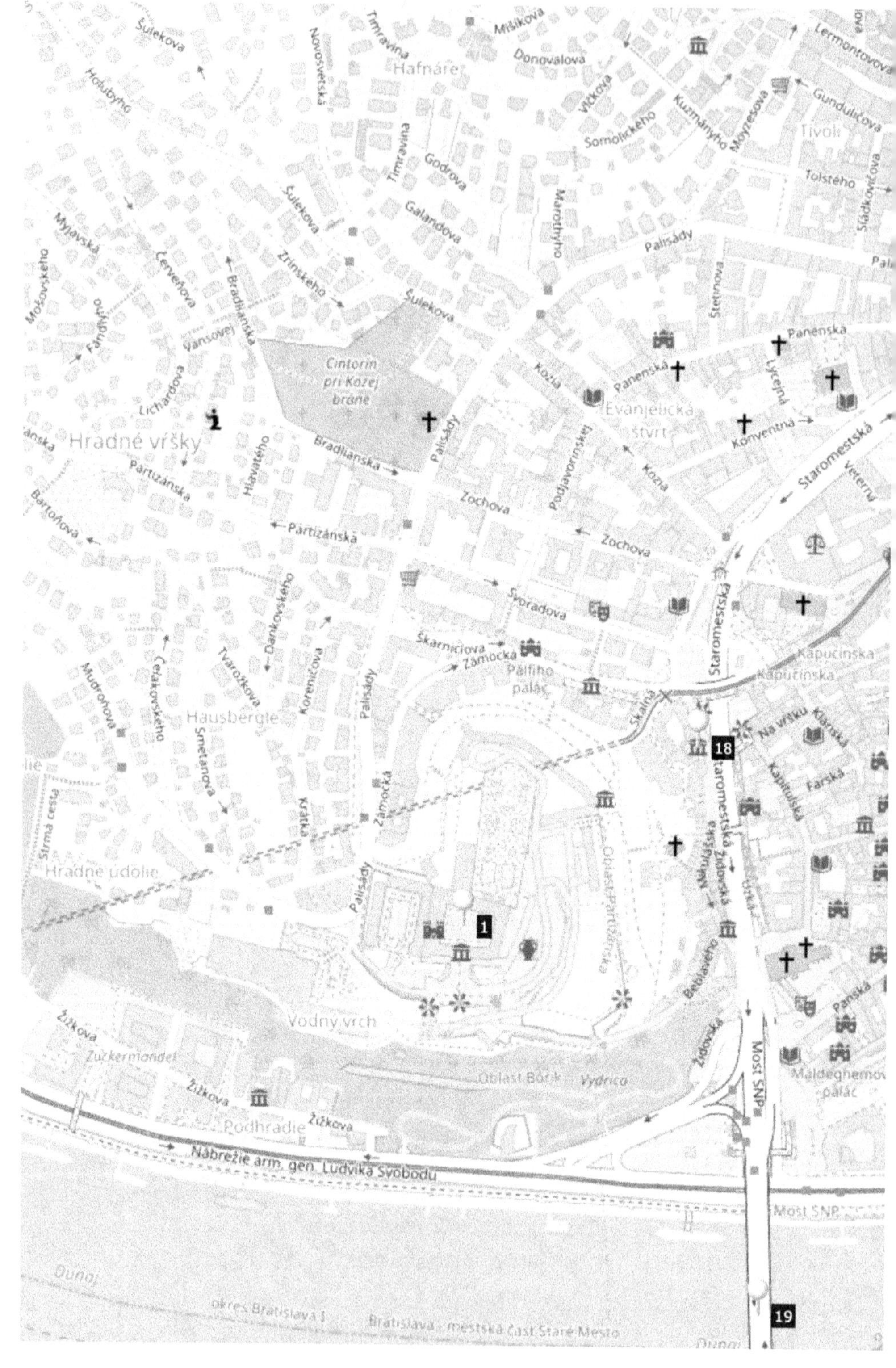

Šulekova
Novosvetská
Timravina
Mišíkova
Hafnáre
Donovalova
Vlčkova
Somolického
Kuzmányho
Moyzesova
Gunduličova
Tivoli
Holubyho
Tolstého
Sladkovičova
Červeňová
Šulekova
Galandova
Godrova
Timravina
Marótbyho
Palisády
Mišovská
Bradlianska
Zrinskeho
Vansovej
Fándlyho
Lichardova
Šulekova
Cintorín pri Kozej bráne
Palisády
Kozia
Panenská
Panenská
Lýcejná
Panenská
Hradné vŕšky
Hlaváťho
Bradlianska
Podjavorinskej
Evanjelická štvrt
Konventná
Staromestská
Partizánska
Zochova
Kozia
Veterná
Battoňova
Partizánska
Zochova
Staromestská
Dankovského
Svoradova
Kapucínska
Čelakovského
Koreničova
Škarniciova
Zámocká
Kapucínska
Mudroňova
Palisády
Pálffiho palác
Na vŕšku
Klariská
Hausbergle
Smetanova
Zámocká
Farská
Kapitulská
Skalná
18
Strmá cesta
Krížna
Palisády
Oblast Partizánska
Prepoštská
Nové schody
Hradné údolie
Beblavého
Zámocká
Žižkova
Palisády
1
Zuckermandel
Vodný vrch
Oblast Bôrik
Vydrica
Židovská
Most SNP
Panská
Maldeghemov palác
Žižkova
Žižkova
Podhradie
Nábrežie arm. gen. Ludvíka Svobodu
Dunaj
okres Bratislava I
Bratislava - mestská časť Staré Mesto
Most SNP
19
Dunaj

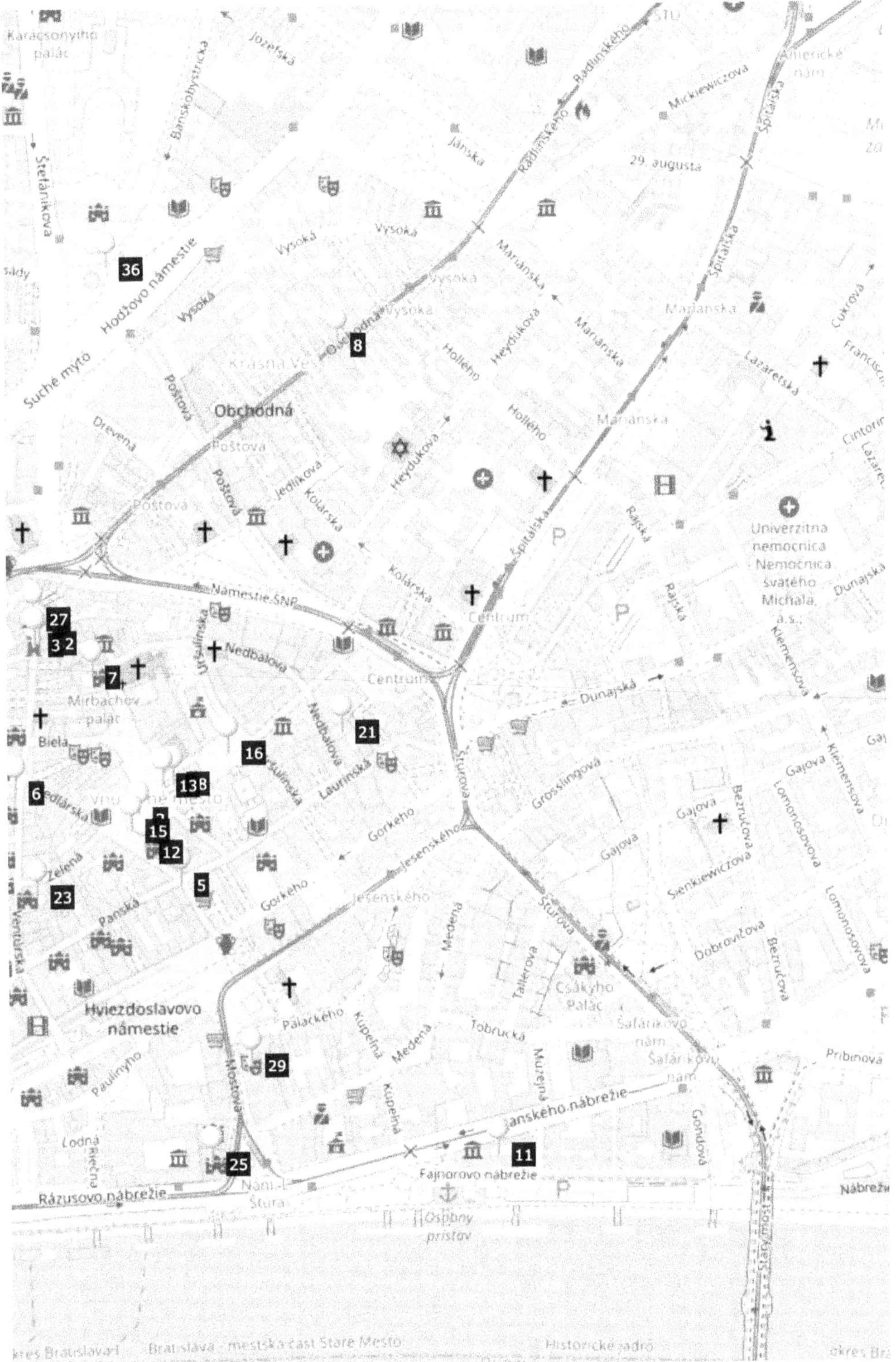

Karácsonyiho palác
Stefánikova
Banskobystrická
Jozefská
Radlinského
Mickiewiczova
Americké nám
Jánska
29. augusta
36
Hodžovo námestie
Vysoká
Vysoká
Vysoká
Vysoká
Mariánska
Mariánska
Spitálska
Lazaretská
Cukrová
Suché mýto
Poštová
Krásna Ves
8
Heydukova
Holého
Mariánska
Cintorín
Lazaretská
Drevená
Obchodná
Poštová
Poštová
Jedlíková
Kolárska
Heydukova
Holého
Spitálska
Rajská
Univerzitná nemocnica
Nemocnica svätého Michala, a.s.
Poštová
Kolárska
P
Dunajská
Námestie SNP
Kolárska
Centrum
Klemensova
27
3 2
Ursulínska
Nedbalova
Centrum
Rajská
P
7
Mirbachov palác
Biela
Nedbalova
Dunajská
21
16
Laurinská
Štúrova
Grösslingova
Gajova
Klemensova
6
Kolárska
Ursulínska
Gorkého
Gajova
Bezručova
Lomonosovova
13 8
Gajova
Sienkiewiczova
15
Jesenského
Štúrova
12
Dobrovičova
Bezručova
Lomonosovova
5
Gorkého
Jesenského
23
Panská
Jesenského
Medená
Štúrova
Ventúrska
Palackého
Kupeľná
Medená
Tobrucká
Csákyho palác
Šafárikovo nám
Hviezdoslavovo námestie
Paulínyho
Medená
Muzejná
Šafárikovo nám
Pribinova
Lodná
Mostová
Kupeľná
...anského nábrežie
Gondova
29
Riečna
11
Lodná
25
Fajnorovo nábrežie
P
Nábrež...
Rázusovo nábrežie
Nám. Štúra
Osobný prístav
okres Bratislava I   Bratislava - mestská časť Staré Mesto
Historické zadrô
okres Bra

Contents

Welcome to Bratislava

The historic city of Bratislava is the capital of Slovakia and is just an hour by car or train from Vienna, Austria. The city of Bratislava is overlooked by a hilltop castle that is set on the banks of the Danube River. As you stroll through Bratislava you'll find lots of shops, old artisans' houses & narrow cobblestone streets. Walk across the chain bridge to Devinska Nova Ves to see the remains of an ancient Roman settlement and visit the Slovak National Theatre with its Art Nouveau facade featuring angels and animals. Check out Bratislava's ornate baroque churches and stop for a morning coffee with sweeping views at the Jan Hus Memorial.

☐ 1. Bratislava Castle

Address: Zámocká 2, 81101 Bratislava, Slovakia

Phone: +421 2 5972 1111

Web: http://www.bratislava-hrad.sk/

Atop an isolated rocky hill of the Little Carpathians stands Bratislava Castle, dominant in the local landscape. First erected in the 13th century and rebuilt several times, it is now home to the National Museum and affords perhaps the best views of the capital city. The castle comprises two parts: a Romanesque keep known as the Dietrichstein Palace and the Gothic palace with its 85 m (280 ft) long hallway added by King Louis II in late Renaissance style.

☐ 2. Main Square

Address: Hlavné námestie, 81101 Bratislava, Slovakia

The history of the Main Square, Bratislava dates back to as early as the 11th century. Located in the very heart of Old Town, it was known by various names through history; it started out as the horse market (1255-1403) and later it became the town hall (16th century). Nowadays this magnificent and monumental square is one of most visited sites in the city. It is a great place to admire magnificent building architecture, historical monuments and amazing ambience of the city.

☐ 3. Michael's Gate

Address: Michalská, 81103 Bratislava, Slovakia

Michael's Gate is the only gate preserved from Bratislava's medieval fortifications. The small town of New Town (Nové Mesto) was established in the 14th century, after King Casimir III of Poland granted it special privileges to become a free trade center. The gate was built around 1300, and remained unchanged until the 17th century when its keystone and the Romanesque portals were destroyed and upgraded with baroque portal and statue of St. Michael from 1758. Michael's Castle is now home to a museum containing top historic weapons, armor, and many other interesting historical exhibits.

☐ 4. UFO Observation Deck

Address: Nový most 1, 81105 Bratislava, Slovakia

Phone: +421 262 5203 00

Email: ufo@redmonkeygroup.com

Web: https://www.instagram.com/ufobratislava/

Web: http://www.u-f-o.sk/

The UFO Observation Deck, Bratislava has become one of the most popular tourist attractions in Slovakia since its opening in 2005. Its unique shape resembling a flying saucer and its breath-taking views attract the attention of many tourists, especially young people who are looking for extreme experiences. The futuristic tower is also an ideal place for lovers, newly wedded couples, as well as for all the visitors wishing to capture a breathtaking picture or spend memorable time with their friends.

☐ 5. Man at Work Statue

Address: 2 Panská, Bratislava 81101, Slovakia

Čumil, also known as "Man at work," is a statue of the man inspired by one of Bratislava's most popular stories — two men witnessed a woman in a local park and couldn't stop talking about it for weeks.

☐ 6. Old Town

Address: 280/22 Ventúrska, Bratislava 81101, Slovakia

The Old Town of Bratislava is a small, historic area with sights to see, restaurants and shops that make for a perfect day trip or afternoon of exploring. Located on the banks of the Danube River, it's one of the most popular places in Slovakia to visit.The Old Town is known for its many churches, including Franciscan Church, Castle Church and St. Martin's Cathedral.

□ 7. Bratislava City Gallery Mirbach Palace

Address: Františkánske nám. 416/11, 815 35 Bratislava, Slovakia
Phone: +421 254 431 556
Email: gmb@gmb.sk
Web: http://www.gmb.sk/

Get to know one of the best Rococo architectural buildings preserved in Slovakia. It was built in 1755 by Carl de Carl for Count Franz Anton von Harrach as a summer palace, on an initiative of the famous baroque Austrian architect Johann Bernhard Fischer von Erlach. The building is today home to the Bratislava City Gallery, offering you a chance to see its fantastic collection of art (both Slovak and international), as well as enjoy temporary exhibitions.

☐ 8. Merchant Street

Address: Obchodná, 81106 Bratislava, Slovakia
Phone: +421 2 6345 2239
Web: https://www.facebook.com/obchodnaulica
Web: http://www.obchodnaulica.sk/en

The Merchant Street in Bratislava is the newest central shopping and entertainment destination of Slovakia. It was awarded the new European Retail Design Award (best shopping street). The street layout was redesigned recently by the famous Italian designer Dante Marchi. The street goes from the Old Town Bridge Tower to St. Michael's Gate (Michael´s Gate) at the end of Michalská Street, beneath Bratislava Castle hill in the Old Town area of Bratislava.

□ 9. Slavín Memorial

Address: 3 Pažického, Bratislava 81104, Slovakia

Wikipedia: https://en.wikipedia.org/wiki/Slavín

The Slavín memorial is composed of a group of monumental concrete sculptures whose central part is dominated by the 25-metre (82 ft) high stylobate, made of red Adriatic marble. The monuments are symbolizing that the capture of Bratislava was a result of cooperation between the Red Army and Czechoslovak troops and their Slovak colleagues from Slovak National Uprising resistance movement.

Slavín is located at an altitude of 541 m (1,777 ft; 109.98 m (362 ft) above sea level) surrounded by a park of 32 hectares (79 acres).

□ 10. Devín Castle

Address: Muránská, 841 10 , Bratislava-Devín, Slovakia

Phone: +421 2 65 73 01 05

Email: mmba@bratislava.sk

The Devín Castle in Bratislava is situated above the right bank of the Danube River, on a high limestone rock that overlooks the place where the Danube River and Morava River join. Surrounded by picturesque natural scenery combined with valuable historical monuments and relics this is one of the most popular tourist destinations in Slovak Republic.

□ 11. Slovak National Museum

Address: Vajanského nábr. 61/2, 81102 Bratislava, Slovakia

Phone: +421 2 204 691 43

The Slovak National Museum is the most important institution focusing on scientific research and cultural education in Slovakia. Its beginnings 'are connected with the endeavour of the Slovak nation for national emancipation and self-determination'. It is headquartered in Bratislava, however, the Slovak National Museum governs 18 specialized museums, most of which are located throughout Slovakia with collections that cover various branches of culture. Each museum has its own area of interest within its particular sphere of influence and expertise.

□ 12. The Handsome Guy Memorial

Address: 355/4 Hlavné námestie, Bratislava 81101, Slovakia

Schöner Náci (The Handsome Guy) was the son of a shoemaker and grandson of a famous clown who was inspired to bring happiness to the streets of the Bratislava.

Schöner Náci was born in Petržalka on August 11, 1897. He had a colorful career as circus artist and soldier. His later years were marked by alcoholism and later tuberculosis, ending with his death on Oct. 23, 1967 in Lehnice. After death, the actor was buried in the village cemetery in Lehnice where his remains are now near a memorial plate and epitaph of the actor who was buried there together with his daughter Ilona Mervó in June 1992.

☐ 13. Old Town Hall

Address: Primaciálne nám. 501/3, 815 18 Bratislava, Slovakia

Phone: +421 259 100 812

Email: mmba@bratislava.sk

A striking symbol of Slovakia's capital, the Old Town Hall is a complex of three townhouses erected in the 14th century. These were connected in the 15th century, resulting in the largest medieval town hall in Central Europe. The tower is the oldest part of the hall; it was constructed around 1370. During its history, it has survived several fires and has been damaged by warfare and its reconstruction always followed the original design preserved in medieval woodcuts.

□ 14. Slovak Radio Building

Address: Mýtna 2826/1, 81107 Bratislava, Slovakia
Phone: +421 2 57273111
Web: http://www.rozhlas.sk/

The Slovak Radio Building is located in Bratislava. It's a building designed by famous local architects Štefan Svetko, Štefan Ďurkovič and Barnabáš Kissling. It was completed in 1983. The project began in 1967. As you see from the picture it is shaped like an upside down pyramid which makes it instantly recognisable.

□ 15. Maximilian Fountain

Address: 356/5 Hlavné námestie, Bratislava 81101, Slovakia

The Roland Fountain, also called the Maximilian Fountain is located in Hlavné námestie (Main Square), in front of the Presidential Palace and northwest of the Old Town Hall. Although its current design and shape are from 1844, it is one of the oldest historical monuments in central Bratislava. The statue on top represents a knight formed after that of Rolando from Verona (Italy).

☐ 16. Primate's Square

Address: 2 Primaciálne námestie, Bratislava 81101, Slovakia

Primate's Square is a connecting passage to the Main Square. It is also bounded by the Primate's Palace on the south, and an ornate building on the east side. On the eastern side of the square lies an arcaded complex that has been refurbished into a Co-working space accommodating several companies including technologists from Austrian and South African firms.

□ 17. Slovak National Theatre

Web: http://www.snd.sk/

The Slovak National Theatre is the oldest in the country. It is located in a Neo-Renaissance theatre in the Old Town and includes a large modern theatre near the Danube.

☐ 18. Museum of Jewish Culture in Slovakia

Address: Židovská ulica 17, 81101 Bratislava, Slovakia
Phone: +421 2 204 90 101
Email: mzk@snm.sk

The Museum of Jewish Culture in Bratislava is the place to learn about Jewish life in Slovakia. It features historical items including from the Holocaust which affected the country terribly in WWII. An exhibit displays photos dedicated to the 70,000 victims from Slovakia as well as clothes, letters, books and religious items.

☐ 19. Bridge of the Slovak National Uprising

Address: Most SNP, 81102, Slovakia

You may be familiar with the Bratislava SNP Bridge, the longest single-span cable-stayed bridge in the world when it was first built. Its nickname of the UFO Bridge (for its resemblance to a flying saucer) comes from its narrow one-pylon span and slender lines. At midcentury the plans were developed for a second parallel bridge, but construction didn't begin until 1990, after the dismantling of the Iron Curtain had begun.

☐ 20. Botanical Garden

Address: Botanická 3, 84104 Bratislava, Slovakia
Phone: 02665425440
Email: jaroslav.bella@rec.uniba.sk

The Botanical Garden of the Comenius University is located near the historic center of Bratislava next to the river Danube and is created for both university research and educational purposes. It contains over 4,000 plant species covering an area of 6.6 hectares. Its two greenhouses are a place suited for exhibits, meetings with the pupils or conferences. The garden houses herbarium, phytotron, seed bank and laboratories where phytochemicals are studied. Everyday it also serves as an open air in-door recreation and relaxation park for students, visitors and locals.

☐ 21. Nedbalka Gallery

Address: 485/15 Nedbalova, Bratislava 81101, Slovakia

Web: https://www.nedbalka.sk/

Nedbalka Gallery focuses on Slovak modern art, ranging from the late-19th century to the present day. Its collection consists of paintings, sculptures and prints. The building itself is an interesting piece of architecture that has been reconstructed to suit the gallery and belongs to one of its kind in Slovakia. The gallery is surrounded by several restaurants located in historic buildings.

☐ 22. Kamzík TV Tower

Address: 14 Snežienková, Bratislava 831 01, Slovakia

The Kamzík TV Tower is situated on a hill near Bratislava Castle with an amazing view of the whole city. The restaurant rotates to offer a 360-degree panoramic view of the whole city. Open for breakfast, lunch, dinner and snacks, this place has become a must-see for tourists visiting Slovakia. We recommend dining at sunset, as there is no better place in Bratislava to see the city lights at night than the Kamzík TV Tower.

☐ 23. Pálffy Palace

Pálffy Palace is a Baroque-style palace in the Old Town. It was built by Count Leopold Pálffy in 1747. Roman and Celtic items were uncovered during archaeological research. The palace once contained a mint and in 1762, Wolfgang Amadeus Mozart played a concert here as a young child.

☐ 24. Golden Sands

Address: Zlaté piesky, 82104 Ružinov, Slovakia

The Golden Sands is the biggest lake of Bratislava and one of the most frequented natural swimming pools for locals. This area is a haven for those seeking to escape the hustle and bustle of city life.

☐ 25. Esterházy Palace

With an ostentatious Neo-Renaissance facade, the Esterházy Palace is one of the most monumental buildings in the Old Town of Bratislava. Built by local architect Karol Machula in the 1870s as the Stolarsky palac, it was reconstructed in the 1920s and, after destruction during World War II, did not reopen until 1994. Today, with the adjacent Water Barracks and modern extension, it hosts some of the Slovak National Gallery exhibitions.

☐ 26. Námestie Slobody

Address: Námestie slobody, Bratislava 81106, Slovakia

Námestie Slobody is one of the most important city squares in Bratislava. It is an ideal place to take a break and relax at one of the cafes or restaurants. The Summer Archbishop's Palace, located at the opposite side of the square, is a prominent example of secession style, built by the famous architect Milan Michal Harminc.

☐ 27. Museum of Pharmacy

The Museum of Pharmacy is housed in an original pharmacy building with its original interior intact. The pharmaceutical memorabilia on display is huge.

☐ 28. Bratislava City Museum

Address: Radničná 1, 81101 Bratislava, Slovakia
Web: http://www.muzeum.bratislava.sk/

The Bratislava City Museum documents the history of Bratislava from the earliest periods until the 20th century. This is the oldest museum in continuous operation in Slovakia.

☐ 29. Slovak Philharmonic

Phone: +421 2 20475 218
Email: filharmonia@filharmonia.sk
Web: http://www.filharmonia.sk/

The Bratislava State Philharmonic is a symphony orchestra that has resided since the 1950s in the Reduta Bratislava concert hall. The orchestra was founded in 1949 and was led by its first principal conductor Bohumil Gregor from 1949 to 1971.

The Slovak Philharmonic is one of the oldest orchestras in Eastern Europe and it has a excellent reputation. Plan your visit to this leading classical music venue to see what all the fuss is about.

☐ 30. Rusovce Mansion

While Rusovce manor house retained traces of its past during the last restoration, today it is one of Bratislava's finest examples of architectural heritage. Its historic interiors exhibit authentic features, allowing for a glimpse into the lifestyle of local magnates and serving as a venue for hosting weddings, meetings and other social gatherings. Outside, a richly decorated garden stretching from the front to the back of the building sets you in a tranquil mood as soon as you step through the gate.

□ 31. ZOO Bratislava

Address: Bratislava 84104, Slovakia
Web: http://www.zoobratislava.sk/

The ZOO Bratislava is the largest and most visited tourist attraction in Slovakia, as well as one of the oldest zoos in Europe. In 1948, it was opened as the first national zoo in a socialist country. The ZOO Bratislava has an area of 97 hectares (250 acres), out of which 35 hectares (89 acres) are open to the public, and is home to over 900 specimens of 175 animal species.

☐ 32. Museum of Arms

Bratislava's Museum of Arms features various weapons and the development of firearms as well as the history of regional fortifications.

Check out the view of the city from the top floor.

☐ 33. Apollo Bridge

Address: Most Apollo, 85101, Slovakia

The Apollo Bridge is a road bridge over the Danube in Slovakia. It is located between the Old Bridge and Harbor Bridge Bridges, a site which allowed almost perpendicular bridging, resulting in the shortest possible span. Construction of the bridge began in 2003 and opened in 2005. It is named for the 'Apollo' oil refinery which was built in 1958 near to where the bridge now stands.

☐ 34. Lanoland Rope Park

Web: https://www.lanoland.sk/

The Lanoland Rope Park includes a climbing wall with 43 knots and 2 bridges in all sizes and difficulty levels suitable for both children and adults. Visitors can choose from 5 routes based on their level of difficulty.

☐ 35. UFO

Address: Bratislava 82106, Slovakia

This UFO once appeared in a Slovakian national park. The strange object was installed by an unknown artist in the middle of the night, drawing crowds to admire and speculate what it is supposed to be and whether it might have actually landed from outer space instead.

☐ 36. Hodžovo námestie Square

Address: 2978/1 Hodžovo námestie, Bratislava 81106, Slovakia

Hodžovo námestie is a major square that is located at the edge of Old Town, in front of the Slovak Presidential Palace.

☐ 37. Harbour Bridge

Address: Prístavný most, Bratislava 82109, Slovakia

The Prístavný most, or "Harbour Bridge" in English, is a double-floor bridge with a railroad and highway across the Danube from Slovakia into Austria. It sits next to the Port of Bratislava, and is a direct route for travelers commuting between Bratislava, Petržalka and Vienna.

☐ 38. Štadión Pasienky

Address: Bratislava 83104, Slovakia

Stadion Pasienky is a multi-purpose stadium in Bratislava, used mostly for football matches as well as other sporting events and concerts.

☐ 39. Church of the Holy Spirit

Web: http://dubravka.fara.sk/

The Church of the Holy Spirit is a wonderful structure. The roof, supported by a pillar in the centre, is made of glass and houses a lift that brings you to the top floor where there are eight bells. It was built in a circular shape and consists of both church and pastoral sections. Look at the unusual glass on the inside. The outside is covered with thousands of yellow glass panels which change colours at different times of day, according to the light intensity.

Picture Credits

Bratislava, Slovakia Cover: danielavaskova / 4793541 (Pixabay)
Bratislava Castle: Groume (CC BY-SA 2.0)
Main Square: Jorge Láscar (CC BY 2.0)
Michael's Gate: Jorge Láscar (CC BY 2.0)
UFO Observation Deck: Hellspawn754 (CC BY-SA 3.0)
Man at Work Statue: Doko (CC BY-SA 3.0)
Old Town: Dguendel (CC BY 3.0)
Bratislava City Gallery Mirbach Palace: Lure (CC BY-SA 3.0)

Merchant Street: Pudelek (GFDL)

Slavín Memorial: Kiwiev (CC0)

Devín Castle: Kirk (CC BY-SA 3.0)

Slovak National Museum: Wizzard (PD)

The Handsome Guy Memorial: Guillaume Speurt (CC BY-SA 2.0)

Old Town Hall: Wizzard (PD)

Slovak Radio Building: Jan Polák (CC BY-SA 3.0)

Maximilian Fountain: Lure (CC BY-SA 3.0)

Primate's Square: Jorge Láscar (CC BY 2.0)

Slovak National Theatre: 23Am.Com (CC BY 2.0)

Museum of Jewish Culture in Slovakia: Wizzard (PD)

Bridge of the Slovak National Uprising: Jay Liu (CC BY 2.0)

Botanical Garden: Mihailo Grbic (CC BY-SA 3.0 rs)

Nedbalka Gallery: Austernfischer Ry (CC BY-SA 4.0)

Kamzík TV Tower: Short Notification Message (CC BY-SA 3.0)

Pálffy Palace: Wizzard (PD)

Golden Sands: Kami (PD)

Esterházy Palace: Wizzard (PD)

Museum of Pharmacy: Solluna (CC BY-SA 3.0)

Bratislava City Museum: Dguendel (CC BY 3.0)

Rusovce Mansion: Lure (CC BY-SA 3.0)

ZOO Bratislava: Stano Novak (CC BY 2.5)

Museum of Arms: Lure (CC BY-SA 3.0)

Apollo Bridge: Toffel (PD)